IMPOSSIBLE
UNLESS YOU
KNOW HOW

OTHER BOOKS BY SHARI LEWIS

The Kids-Only Club Book
Spooky Stuff
How Kids Can Really Make Money
Toy Store In A Book
Magic for Non-Magicians
The Tell It-Make It Book
Folding Paper Puppets, with Lillian Oppenheimer
Folding Paper Toys, with Lillian Oppenheimer
Folding Paper Masks, with Lillian Oppenheimer
Making Easy Puppets
Fun with the Kids
Dear Shari
Be Nimble, Be Quick, with Jacquelyn Reinach
Knowing and Naming, with Jacquelyn Reinach
Thinking and Imagining, with Jacquelyn Reinach
Looking and Listening, with Jacquelyn Reinach

IMPOSSIBLE
UNLESS YOU
KNOW HOW

By Shari Lewis
Illustrated by Victoria Clark
Art Direction by John Brogna

Holt, Rinehart and Winston
New York

Acknowledgment

Kids-Only Club Book Series advisor is Dr. A.B. Hurwitz, formerly Peter Pan the Magic Man, the official magician for the City of New York.

Published by Holt, Rinehart and Winston, 383 Madison Avenue, New York, New York 10017. Published simultaneously in Canada by Holt, Rinehart and Winston of Canada, Limited.

Library of Congress Cataloging in Publication Data

Lewis, Shari.
    Impossible, Unless You Know How.
    (Kids-Only Club)
    Includes index.
    SUMMARY: Includes riddles and tricks with which to entertain friends.
    1. Tricks — Juvenile literature.   2. Riddles — Juvenile literature.   [1. Magic tricks.   2. Riddles]
I. Clark, Victoria.   II. Title.
GV1548.L49   793.8   79-2357
ISBN 0-03-049681-0
ISBN 0-03-049686-1 pbk.

Printed in the United States of America
10   9   8   7   6   5   4   3   2   1

Dedication

Jeremy Tarcher is amazing. He figures out
how tricks and stunts are done before you're
finished doing them. No one has ever known
this about Jeremy Tarcher. Now the world
will know. Jeremy Tarcher is my husband and
my friend and I'm happy to dedicate this book
to him.

CONTENTS

FOTO FUN

Shawn   Barker

Jimmy

Georgia   Mally

Twerp

8

Introduction

Some people are Impossible nuts. No, I don't mean that they are impossible *nuts*, I mean they're nuts about those tricky stunts that seem impossible to do. *I* like challenges like that as long as they're not impossible for *me* to do, because I know the secret!

This is a book full of secrets. Some are "betchas," pranks that only you can pull, because only you know that special little something. Others are "betcha can'ts" — dares that no one will believe, because what you are claiming is *impossible* to do seems so simple. Well, just let 'em try!

Of course, there's an old poem that goes:

> Don't say a thing's impossible
> The chances are you'll rue it,
> 'Cause someone else may come along
> And find a way to *do* it!

The Kids-Only Club gang — Shawn, Georgia, Jimmy, Mally, and Twerp love it when they know how to do things that no one else can do. If you agree, you'll find lots of your kind of fun in IMPOSSIBLE, UNLESS YOU KNOW HOW.

1
Do You Know
The Secret?

These "betchas" work because you are a step ahead of your pals. You alone know the sneaky way to meet the challenge. Practice each stunt at least once in private before you do it for real live people.

Do it for the dog.

Watch yourself do it in the mirror.

Then you'll not only *know* the secret, but you'll be able to make it work for you!

SWITCH!

Ask your friend to hold his or her arms out sideways, parallel to the floor, and to make them stiff. Put a book in one of your pal's hands and say, "I'll betcha you can't transfer that book to the other hand without bending your arms either at the elbow or at the shoulder." Most likely, your friend won't be able to do it. But you will! Here's the secret:

Hold your arms out in that same position, with the book in one hand. Switch the book to the other hand by bending your knees, tilting your body, and plopping the book down on a table. Then turn your body so that your other arm is facing the table. Once again, bend your knees and tilt your body (keep those arms stiff). Then pick up the book in your other hand!

FOUR FROM FOUR

Can you take away 4 and leave 8? In other words, how is it possible to take 4 from 4, and still be left with 8?

Secret: take a square piece of paper, and tear off the four corners — you will end up with eight corners! If we were

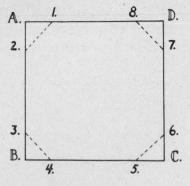

to tear off the original four corners in the picture (A, B, C, and D), we'd be left with eight new ones!

STRONG FINGER, WEAK FISTS

Say to your friend, "Put one fist on top of the other." When your pal has done that, say, "I'll betcha I can knock your fists apart with one finger." Then, with your pointer finger, stroke (gently hit) your friend's top fist right off the bottom one!

Now you say, "I'll betcha you can't do that to me." You put one fist on top of the other, and your pal cannot knock them apart!

Here's the secret:

When you put one fist on top of the other, stick the thumb of your bottom hand up into the top fist and grip it tightly for support. (Don't let anyone see you doing this!) Strike as he or she will, your friend won't be able to separate your fists.

CRAZY COINS

A trickster who knows a couple of stunts that can be done with coins is always ready for action. You can reach into your pocket anytime, anywhere, and pull out your props. Three of these crazy coin betchas are line-'em-ups, two are puzzling coin games (that you can always win), and one will make you seem like a detective, since you can figure out the solution based on a secret fact that most people don't happen to know. The last, Catchy Coins, is a juggling stunt.

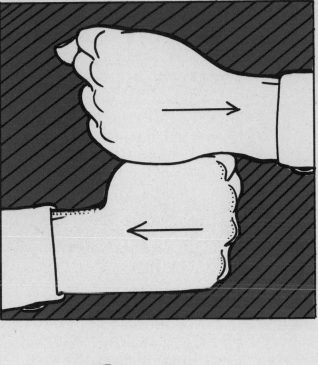

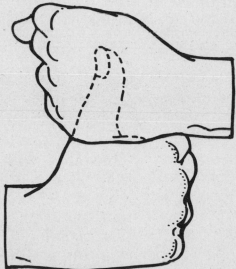

Line-'em-ups

• Start with six coins. To make two rows of three coins each is easy, but can you make two rows of four coins each? Two ways are possible.

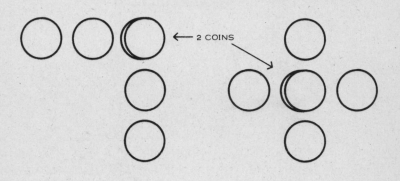

2 COINS

• Place twelve coins in a square so that there are four coins in each row.

Now, can you move these coins into another figure that has *five* coins in each row?

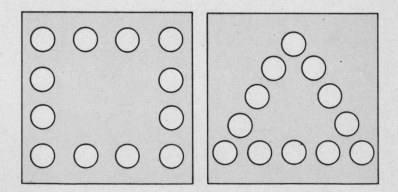

- Lay six coins so that they are touching one another in two rows, three on top, three on the bottom, as in the picture.

Can you change these two rows of coins into a circle of six coins in only three moves? The rules are: Handle only one coin at a time without moving any other. When a coin is moved, it must still touch two other coins in its new position.

Secret: First move penny A so that it's on top of (and touching) pennies B and C. Next, move B so that it rests on top of D and E. Last, shift penny D so that it is in between A and B.

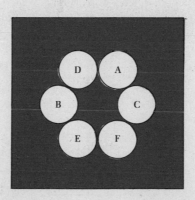

Coin Games

- This is a puzzle if you don't know how, a game if you do.

Start by drawing a tall rectangle. Make four horizontal lines (side to side) across the inside of the rectangle, dividing it into five boxes, one on top of another. Put one penny in the top box, and one in the second. Leave the third box empty. Put a nickel in the fourth box and a nickel in the fifth.

The object is to move the pennies into the nickel boxes, and the nickels into the penny boxes — with only eight moves. Either a slide of a coin from one box to another or a jump over another coin (as in checkers) is considered one move.

Try it, and then (and only then) do I give you permission to read the solution.

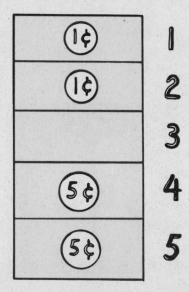

The secret moves:

1. Slide a penny from box 2 into box 3.
2. Jump the nickel from box 4 into box 2.
3. Slide the nickel from box 5 into box 4.
4. Jump the penny from box 3 into box 5.
5. Jump the penny from box 1 into box 3.
6. Slide the nickel from box 2 into box 1.
7. Jump the nickel from box 4 into box 2.
8. Slide the penny from box 3 into box 4.

1.   2.   3.   4.   5.   6.

• Place six coins on a table so that the first three are heads up, the next three, tails up. Can you turn the coins over — *two at a time* — so that they wind up alternating heads-tails-heads-tails-heads-tails?

Here's the secret:

First turn over coins 3 and 4. Then turn over coins 4 and 5. Now turn over coins 2 and 3. Congratulations! You now have your coins heads-tails-heads-tails-heads-tails.

Coin Detective

• How can you tell a penny from a dime and a nickel from a quarter when the coins are in your pocket or when you are in the dark?

Here's the secret:

A penny has a smooth edge, a dime has a ribbed one. A nickel has a smooth edge, but a quarter has a ribbed one.

Catchy Coins

This juggling stunt will really impress your friends, and it's so simple that you should be able to do it by the third try.

Holding your hand palm up, place a little pile of coins on your elbow. Cup your hand, so it forms a little pocket aimed at your elbow. Now drop your elbow (suddenly and with a smooth circular swing of your arm). This will bring your hand to just below where your elbow was, and you'll catch the pile of coins.

It won't work the first time, but by the second or third, you'll find that you'll be able to catch the coins neatly and cleanly.

The real secret is not to throw the coins either up or out, but just to *sweep the hand down and drop the elbow* quickly out from under the coins. *Your hand will simply be where the coins are.* If you haven't gotten it by the second try, bend your knees a little as you do the stunt.

Keep track of how many coins you end up catching. Perhaps you can even break the world's record!

TRICKS WITH STICKS

All of these stunts can be done with toothpicks, cotton swab sticks, paper clips, blades of grass, or whatever sticks you have on hand.

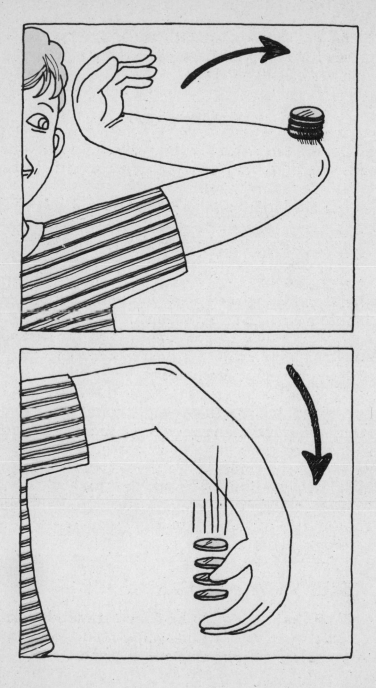

• This pattern of thirteen squares is made with thirty-six sticks. Can you remove just eight sticks so that you wind up with a pattern of six squares instead of the original thirteen?

The Secret:

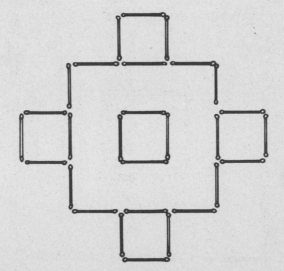

• Place twenty-four sticks so that they form nine squares. Can you take away eight sticks, leaving only two squares?

The Secret:

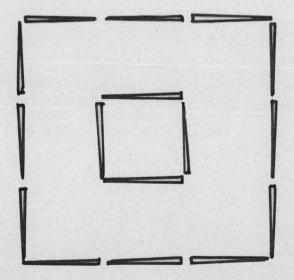

• This one is best done with cotton swab sticks. You say, "Can you lift three cotton swab sticks with a fourth? I can." And when your friend gives up, here's how you do it:

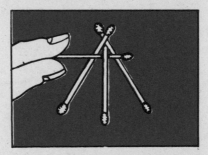

• With twelve sticks, form four squares. Can you rearrange them to make three squares by only moving three sticks? (Don't remove *any* sticks.)

The Secret:

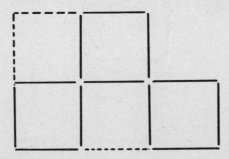

WATER, WATER EVERYWHERE

"Water, water everywhere but not a drop to drink" — unless your friends figure out how to do this stunt.

Put a glass full of water on a table, cover it with a saucer, and then top the saucer with an empty glass. Say, "I'll betcha you can't drink that glass of water, using only one hand, which may not touch the saucer."

Let each of your friends try to solve this problem, and when no one can, then show them the solution.

Put two flat-topped chairs back to back. Pick up the bottom glass (which will automatically lift the saucer and the top glass). Slip this bottom glass between the two chair backs. This will slide the saucer along the top of the two chairs so that it rests on the backs, supporting the top glass. Now you can remove the bottom glass and drink it to the last drop.

2
Groaners

Some stunts make folks grin. Others make 'em groan. Do you like groaners? Those are the dumb gags and sucker bets that have jerky, jokey solutions (like the one where you say to a pal, "I'll bet you a quarter you can't take off your coat alone." And then, as soon as your friend starts taking off his or her coat, you just take off your coat, too.)

Friends always groan when you tell them groaners — and then they turn around and pull the same gag on the very next person they meet! Here are a baker's dozen (that's twelve plus one) of dopey dares.

1. Say to a friend: "I'll betcha I can stay under water for a full minute." And when your friend forks up a dime to cover that bet, you simply fill a glass with water and place it over your head.

2. Challenge someone: "I'll betcha you can't say fish with your mouth closed." And when they are all done doing rotten imitations of a

ventriloquist, you simply say, "Fish with your mouth closed."

3. You can bet anybody this: "I can stick out my tongue and touch my ear." And then all you do is stick out your tongue, and (with your hand) touch your ear.

4. Or you can boast: "I'll betcha I can jump across the street" — and then what you do is go across the street and jump a couple of times.

5. You say to your pal: "Give me a penny, and without looking at it, I'll be able to tell you the date." And unless your pal has heard this trick before, he or she will give you a penny and will expect to be told the date on it. But what you'll do is tell your friend the date of *that day*. After all, you never said you were going to tell your pal the date on the penny, did you?

6. Get a friend into the kitchen. On the table have butter, eggs, and all the other things that a person needs to make an omelet, together with a frying pan. (I'm just assuming your kitchen has a stove as well.)
Say, "I'll betcha that you can't make an omelet with these ingredients. In fact, I'll betcha that the best cook in the world will not be able to make an omelet with them." Your friend will discover you're right when he or she breaks open the eggs and finds that you boiled them ahead of time, so that they are *very* hard!

7. Bet somebody ten dollars that he or she can't answer "a hard boiled egg" to three questions that you'll ask. First ask any two silly questions that you can think of. Your third question should be, "Which would you rather win, this ten-dollar bet or a hard-boiled egg?" If your friend says, "A hard-boiled egg," hand over the hard-boiled egg. If your friend says, "The ten dollars," he or she loses the bet and the money!

8. Can you read minds? No? I can't either, but when I was a kid I used to pretend I could.

I'd say to a friend, "I'm going to read your mind." And then I'd make a motion on a pad of paper as though I were writing what the other person was thinking. What I was actually writing on the paper was the word "No," but when I wrote it, I'd move my hand around the paper so my friend couldn't tell what I was scribbling.

Then I'd say, "Do you know what I wrote on this piece of paper?" The other person would, of course, say, "No," and then I'd triumphantly say, "I read your mind — I knew you were going to say that! See?" And I'd turn my pad around and show my pal that "No" was exactly what I had written on the piece of paper.

9. You can make this claim: "I can have you clasp your hands together in such a way that it will be impossible for you to leave the room without unclasping your hands." Here's how you can do it: Clasp your pal's hands around a pole, a piano leg, or anything unmovable.

10. Tell the group that your pencil has a special magic point. If someone will name a color, your pencil will write that color. Let us say that a person names "red." What you do is write the *word* "red" on the piece of paper, and indeed, your pencil *did* write that color!

Make sure that when you finish this trick you take a very deep bow. That's the only way you'll avoid being hit by the things your friends will throw at you.

11. Say to a friend: "I'll betcha that I have a piece of paper with some handwriting on it for which you would quickly pay ninety-five cents. And when your friend argues, simply pull out a dollar bill and point to the signature of the Secretary of the Treasury.

12. Then say: "I'll betcha that I can stand on the same piece of newspaper that you're standing on, and you won't be able to touch me, even though I'm only a few inches away." When your friend gives up, spread a sheet of newspaper over the door sill, close the door most of the way, and you and your friend will be in different

rooms. You can stand on the same paper, but he
or she will not be able to touch you through the
almost closed door.

13. Bet someone that you can reel off a thousand words without using the letter *A*. (Reeling off even a hundred words without an *A* would be considered quite an accomplishment, since *A* is the third most frequently used letter in the alphabet.) What your friend doesn't know is that you are about to count from 1 to 999. There are no *A*s in the number system until you get to 1000!

3
Get the
Picture?

People confidently say, "When I see it, I'll believe it," but that's not necessarily so. You can't always believe your eyes because your eyes can be tricked — by shapes, by shadows, and even by suggestions from your mind, which often insists on seeing what it *thinks* it should be seeing.

Here are some stunts that will make your friends say, "I can't believe my eyes!"

UP A TREE

What is this?

Answer: A bear climbing a tree. (Get it? The bear's around the other side and all we can see are the four paws.)

Try To Picture This

Just think about this one: If you take a rectangle of paper and fold it in half and then again in the same direction and then a third time, how many creases will be on that piece of paper when you open it up?

Answer: Seven creases.

THE MISSING ARROW

Adding only two straight lines, can you make a third arrow just like the two in the picture?

Answer:

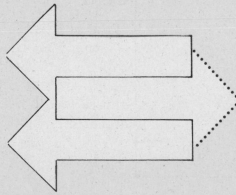

PENNY FOR YOUR THOUGHTS

Say to a friend: "Do you have a penny? Look at it. Now look at the table top in this picture. It looks bigger than a penny, doesn't it? Want to bet? I'll betcha there's no way that you can put your penny down on the table in this picture without the sides of the penny touching the edges of the tabletop." (There's no trick to this — it can't be done. The size of the tabletop is an optical illusion.)

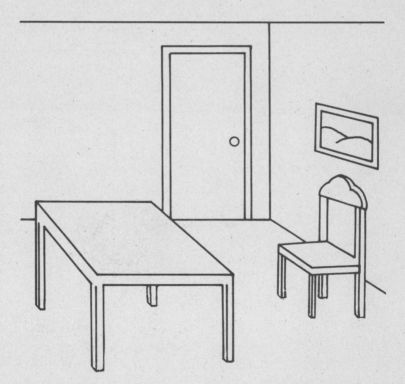

BAFFLING BOXES

Can you cross off six lines to make ten?
Here's how it can be done:

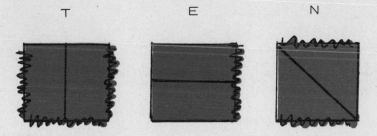

Now you can draw squares like this and stump your friends.

1000 THE HARD WAY

Betcha can't write 1000 in numbers without lifting your pencil from the paper. Give up? Here's how it's done:

Fold down a flap at the top of a sheet of paper. Draw the "1" of the 1000 so that it extends past the edge. Without lifting your pencil, continue the line up onto the flap for a loop. That will become the first "0." Do the same for the next two "0"s.

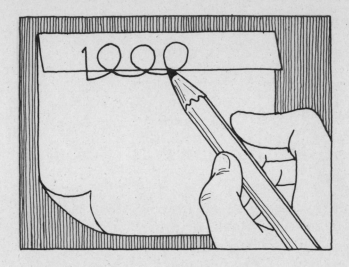

Now lift the flap and you have done your 1000 without lifting your pen from the paper.

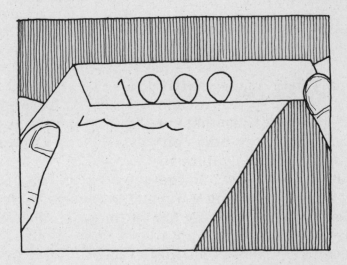

4
Mysteries

Here are some detective stories for you to tell to
your friends. But first you have to solve them, so
get your thinking cap and your wrinkled rain-
coat and read on.

THE ESCAPE

Two friends are in the same jail cell. They're
desperately looking for a way to escape. Their
cell has no windows — just a skylight with no
bars. They know that if they can get to the
skylight, they can escape through it. Unfortu-
nately, it's so high that even when they stand on
each other's shoulders on the bed (which is the
only piece of furniture in the room) they can't
reach the skylight. So they take one of the bed
legs and start to dig a tunnel. Soon they realize
that they'll have to dig too far to escape. Just as
they're about to give up, one of them shouts, "I
have it!" What was his idea? What did they do?
How did they escape?

You now have all the clues.

Solution: They dug a tunnel in order to gather lots of dirt above the ground. And then they piled the dirt up, climbed on top of that mountain of dirt, reached the skylight, and escaped!

THE KIDNAPPING

This is a famous old mystery. It starts in New York City. After washing up, a boy gets into bed and falls asleep. In the morning, he wakes up and goes into his bathroom. Everything looks exactly the same. But when he turns on the water to take a bath, he knows that he has been kidnapped. He is *definitely* not in the same place. In fact, he can see that he has been spirited to a very distant place.

How does he know?

Roll the clues around your brain for a moment before you read the solution.

Solution: When the boy turns on the water for his morning bath, he can see the water swirling down the drain *counterclockwise*. North of the equator the water always swirls down the drain *clockwise*. (And as an ex-New Yorker I can assure you that New York is and has always been north of the equator.) So when, on this particular morning, the boy notices the counterclockwise motion of the water, that means that he has been spirited away to South America or Australia, or some other place south of the equator.

SLOW BOAT

A man wished to buy the slowest boat made in the United States. He placed an advertisement to that effect in the local paper. Three captains answered his ad. To decide which boat was the slowest, he told the three captains to race across the lake and back. The three set out. By the end of the day, none of them had come back. Each was trying to prove that his boat was the slowest.

How should the man have arranged the race to find out which boat really was the slowest?

Solution: The man should have asked each captain to pilot *another* boat, not his own. Then each captain would have been sure to go as fast as possible in this other boat in order to prove that his own boat was the slowest.

THE MASKED MAN

A man is running toward home. Suddenly he encounters a masked man. He quickly stops and begins running back where he started. Where are they? What happened?

Solution: The man running is in a baseball game. He is running from third base to home and is met by a catcher wearing a catcher's mask. The runner stops and races back to third base.

"DON'T SHOOT ME, JOHN"

Several shots are heard just after a voice says pleadingly, "Don't shoot me, John." When the police get into the room, they find a lawyer, a doctor, an army lieutenant, and a milkman. A gun is on the floor. The police immediately arrest the milkman. What could there be about the lawyer, doctor, and lieutenant that makes the police so sure that the milkman was the one who fired the gun?

Solution: The lawyer, doctor, and army lieutenant are women. The only person who could logically have been called John is the milkman.

WHAT HAPPENED HERE?

When you try this mystery on your friends, you can only say yes or no in answer to their questions. No explanations!

Say to your friends, "The mystery is this: Jack walks into the house, heads for the den, opens the door, and here is what he sees: The window is open. Water and broken glass are on the floor. Sam and Mary are lying there, dead. What happened?"

No! Don't read on — try to figure it out.

Give up?

Solution: A hurricane blew the fish tank off the table, onto the floor, breaking it and spilling the water. Sam and Mary? They are fish.

CLEAN AND DIRTY

Two miners came out of a coal shaft. One came out dirty; the other was clean. The one who was clean went over to a pump and washed himself. Strangely enough, the one who was dirty went home without washing. How can you account for this?

Solution: The dirty miner looked at the clean miner, assumed he was clean too, and didn't think it was necessary for him to wash himself.

THE BUS DRIVER

You're driving a bus, and 32 people get on. Then 14 people get off. Then 130 people get on. Next, 9 people get off. Then 2 people get on and 120 people get off. At the next stop 19 people get on. Finally, 36 people get off.

The question is this: What color are the bus driver's eyes?

Solution: The bus driver's eyes are whatever color your eyes are. After all, the first thing I said was, "You're driving a bus!"

DOUBLE TROUBLE

Two boys fill out registration forms for summer camp. The registrar sees that they have the same parents, live at the same address and have the same date of birth. The only difference is that one is named Tony and the other is Adam. When asked, "Are you twins?" they both say, "No." If their answers are accurate and they both have the same mother and father, how can they not be twins?

Solution: Tony and Adam are two of a set of triplets.

THE GRATEFUL COWBOY

This mystery isn't really a hard nut to crack. It's a scene from an old Western movie. A cowboy walks into a bar. The bartender pulls out a gun, and the cowboy says, "Thank you!" Why?

Solution: The man who walked into the bar had the hiccups, and the bartender pulled the gun to scare the cowboy out of his hiccups.

THE ELEVATOR ENIGMA

A man gets into an elevator and pushes the button. He goes to the main floor, gets out, and goes to work. At the end of the day, when he comes home, he gets into the same elevator, pushes a button, goes to the fifth floor and walks up two more stories. Why?

Solution: The man is a midget. He could reach the low button for the main floor, but he lives on the seventh and can't reach up to the button for his own floor.

THE MOVIE THEATER SURPRISE

Mrs. Lindo left the movie theater and walked toward the unlighted parking lot where she had left her car. There were no artificial lights or moonlight, yet she was able to spot her car about seventy-five yards away. How come she could see it?

Solution: She had been to an afternoon show and it was broad daylight.

THE MONEY MYSTERY

A teacher was giving a lesson in how to make change with different coins. One student had $1.15, but each time he was asked to make change he said, "Sorry, I can't do it." After hearing this several times, the teacher became annoyed and went to look at the money. Surprisingly, he was right.

— He had no dollars (paper or silver).
— He couldn't change a half-dollar coin.

— He couldn't break a quarter.

— Even for a dime, he couldn't make change.

— Neither did he have change for a nickel.

What coins *did* George have that added up to $1.15?

Solution: George's money consisted of four dimes, a quarter, and a half-dollar.

THE DRY DIAMOND

Mrs. Honeyfinger was working in the kitchen when her diamond ring slipped off her finger and fell smack into some coffee. Strange to say, the diamond did not get wet. Why not?

Solution: The ring fell into a can of dry ground coffee.

5
Do You Have the
Magic Touch?

My daddy is a magician. Really! While I was growing up, he was the official magician for the City of New York. On stage, people called him Peter Pan the Magic Man. He's taught me some good — and easy — tricks. I'll share a couple with you.

MEALTIME MIRACLE

You put a cup, a fork, a spoon, and a saucer on the table in that order, going from left to right. You tell your friend to choose any one of the objects mentally, but not to tell you which was picked. Then, as you tap the objects with a pencil, your pal is to *silently spell the name of the object*, one letter to each tap, and say "Stop" at the last letter. Your pencil will be resting on the very object that your pal secretly picked. (For example, if the cup was chosen, your friend would think *C* on the first tap, *U* on the second, and your pencil would be pointing to the cup as your friend got to think *P*.)

Here's how it works: The objects are spelled with three, four, five, or six letters. (Cup is three, fork is four, spoon is five, saucer is six.) You make the first two taps on *any* object. You then go from left to right, tapping each object once. As the last letter is silently spelled by your friend, you will be tapping the object he or she picked. So if the word was *CUP*, the C and U would be tapped anywhere, but on P you'd have gone to the object on the left, which is the cup.

THE NEW SHELL GAME

Here's how you can play the shell game as a game or as a trick.

Start with three paper cups and one cookie. Place the cookie under one of the cups and switch the cups around so that your friends can't tell which cup has the cookie. The game is this: Whoever guesses where the cookie is keeps it.

That'll be fun for your friends, but here's the way you can make it *magic* and even more fun:

Beforehand, glue a single hair from your head to the lip of one cup. The hair, which no one else will see, will make it possible for you to keep your eye on that cup. Place the cookie under it and then let your friends rearrange all the cups as quickly as they can, trying to confuse you. You will always be able to tell exactly where that cookie is.

COOKIE

HAIR

THE STICKY SOLUTION

Do your folks constantly complain that you make money disappear faster than they can earn it? Would you like to show them that you can magically change four coins into five? That'll sure stop them!

Here's how it works: Before you do this trick, hide a coin under the edge of a table. Stick it there with a bit of soap, a tiny blob of chewing gum, or a drop of rubber cement.

When your parents are ready, roll up your sleeves and place four coins on the table. Now cup your right hand just below the table. With your left hand, brush the four coins into your right hand and close it.

Now ask Mom and Dad to blow on your hand. Then slowly open your fingers and show five coins instead of four!

The secret is simple. As the coins were being pushed into your right hand, the fingers of that hand were reaching under the table and picking up the hidden coin.

Tell Mom and Dad that money made in this way doesn't even have to be declared on the family's income tax.

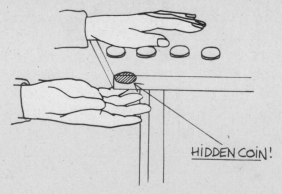

HIDDEN COIN!

SUM TRICK!

Have your pal write down any two numbers, one under the other. Ask your friend to add these two numbers, and put the sum under them. Say, "Continue to add the sum of the last two numbers and write that sum under the other numbers. Keep this up until there are ten numbers in

```
   1
   5
   6
  11
  17
  28
  45 × 11 = 495
  73
 118
 191
─────
 495
```

the column." (On my list of numbers I have 1 and 5, which equals 6. Then I add the 5 and 6, which comes to 11. The 6 and 11 make 17, and so on.)

Now tell your friend, "Add up the column of ten numbers as fast as you can." The surprising thing is that before your friend gets very far, you'll know the answer. Can you figure out how you'll do this?

Here's how: Just multiply the *seventh* number in the row by 11, and you will get the sum of ten numbers, no matter what those numbers are!

And here's the shortest shortcut to multiplying low two-digit numbers by 11: Just add the two digits together, and put the sum in the middle. (So, to multiply 45 by 11, I added the 4 and the 5, and put the 9 in the middle, to get 495.) See page 91 to find a shortcut for multiplying two high-digit numbers by 11.

PICK A NUMBER

Copy this box full of numbers onto a 3 x 5 card or piece of paper and take it to school with you. You'll be able to do one of the best number-tricks I have ever seen.

Say to a friend, "Think of any number on this chart. Tell me which vertical (up and down) rows you find it in. If you find it in more than one row, tell me that, too. And I will tell you the number you thought of."

Here's how you do it: Memorize the numbers at the top of each vertical column (there are four of them — 1, 2, 4, and 8). When your friend tells you the rows the selected number is in, add all the top numbers in those rows. For example, if your pal picked 5, 5 is found in the first and third rows. The number at the top of the first row is 1, the number at the top of the third row is 4. You add 1 and 4 and you get 5, which is the number that your friend thought of.

1	2	4	8
7	6	13	10
5	3	15	14
3	15	7	13
11	7	6	15
9	10	5	12
13	14	12	11
15	11	14	9

Okay — here's one more example. The number 15 is in all four rows. So you add up the four numbers at the top of the four rows — 1 + 2 + 4 + 8 and you get 15. Good, huh?

CONCENTRATION

Say to a friend, "This trick takes concentration. First, think of a number. Double it (I'll wait). Add 10. Divide the total that you get by 2. Now subtract the number you started with. Your answer will be 5."

Your answer will always be 5, no matter what number you think of first. For example, if you started by thinking of the number 2, here's what you get:

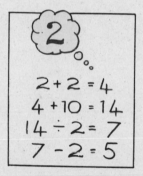

2 + 2 = 4
4 + 10 = 14
14 ÷ 2 = 7
7 - 2 = 5

Try this trick on your friends. They'll be amazed. Are you amazed? Here's the simple, not-so-amazing-if-you-know-the-secret-reason why the answer will always be 5: After you think of a number and double it, the number that you add can be any *even* number. The answer to the trick will always be *half* of that even number. (We added 10, so the answer had to be 5.)

For example, you could add 20 instead, and then the trick would run like this (let's start with the number 3, just for the fun of it):

$$3 + 3 = 6$$
$$6 + 20 = 26$$
$$26 \div 2 = 13$$
$$13 - 3 = 10$$

If you do this trick over and over for your friends, you can really confuse them by picking a *different even number to add* everytime.

PICK THE DATE

Remember this one the next time you have a calendar handy. Ask your pal to pick any seven-day row of numbers on the calendar. Say, "I'll add up the sum of that week of dates faster than you can!" On the word "go," all you do is take the lowest number in that row and add three to it. Then multiply the answer you get by seven. You'll have the sum of those seven dates faster than your friend, unless your pal's a whiz. For example, if, say, the second week in January starts with the number 7, 7 plus 3 equals 10, and 10 times 7 equals 70. And if you add up the dates of that week, 7, 8, 9, 10, 11, 12, 13, you get 70.

THE MAGIC FINGER

Here's a trick that may convince your friends that you are magical right to your fingertips.

Cut a soda straw in half and put one of the halves on a table in front of you. Say, "I'll magnetize the straw by drawing a circle around it with my pointer finger, and as I move that finger away the straw will follow it." Yes, it will — 'cause here's the secret:

Draw the circle around the straw with your finger. Do it three times. Lower your head as you do, watching the straw closely and positioning your head about twelve inches from the straw. Hold your lips slightly apart. After you circle, move your finger away from you and, at that moment, gently blow on the straw so that it follows your finger. Just make sure that your lips don't move as you blow. And for goodness sake, blow without making any noise.

THE TALKING CARD

As a ventriloquist, people think I can make anything talk. Here's a card trick that will give you a reputation as a ventriloquist as well as a magician, because the cards will talk to you.

Before you start, sneak a peek at the top card of your deck. Then shuffle, keeping that top card on the top. Put the pack on your left hand and hold your right hand out, palm up. Tell your friend to cut the pack in half, placing the other half on your right hand. (You now have the top half of the deck on your right, the bottom half on your left.)

Tell your friend to take any card. If your friend takes the top card from the pile on your right hand, you can name it. (Why not? After all, it is the same card that was on the top of the deck, and you memorized that one.)

If your friend takes any other card in the entire deck (from either pile), tell him or her to touch that chosen card to the top of the pile in your right hand, and then to put the card to your ear. It is absolutely amazing, but the card your friend chose is going to tell you the name of the top card in that pile.

And when your friend turns over that top card and sees that you've guessed it correctly, don't forget to say "thank you" to the card that "talked" and helped you do the trick.

AN EYE AT THE END OF YOUR FINGER

Say to someone, "You can't tell, but I have an eye at the end of my finger." Give the person a pack of cards to shuffle. Take them back and put them in your pocket. Then, by sense of touch alone, call out the name of each card, one at a time, before you take it out of your pocket and show it.

Here's how: Before you do this trick, take five cards from the deck, memorize the order in which you're holding them, and put them in your pocket in that order. (Don't let anyone see you do this!)

When the time comes to do your show, take the deck back from the person who shuffled it and put it in your pocket so it's right under the five cards which you already have in your pocket. Then reach in, name the top card (which you have memorized), and take it out and show it to everyone. You can repeat this with the next four.

If you don't stop after five cards, your fingers are on their own!

FLAP, FLAP

This is an absolutely amazing trick, and if you don't tell anyone, no one will know that it's so.

Shuffle a deck of cards, then ask your friend to count any number of cards from the top of the deck down into a pile on the table. Tell your pal to count the same number of cards into a second pile. (So let's say your pal counted ten cards down into the first pile. He or she would then have counted ten cards into the second pile as well.)

Now say, "Cut either pile to any card, remember the bottom card that you've cut to, and put the group of cards in your hand on top of the other pile. Now put the rest of the cards from the first pile on top of the second pile as well." In other words, let's pretend that your friend cut the first pile to the third card. (And we'll pretend that the third card was the ace of hearts.) Your

friend would have memorized that card. Then those three cards would not have been put back on the first pile (from which they came) but rather onto the other. In addition, your pal would now pick up all the rest of that first pile and put those cards on top of the other pile, as well. Got it?

At this point, you, the magician, turn the cards over one at a time, and when you get to the card picked and memorized by your friend, you know exactly which it is.

Here's how you do it: Secretly, when your friend counts the first group of cards into a pile, you listen to the cards flapping onto the table and remember how many cards were put down into that pile. And at the very end of the trick, when you have the deck in front of you, you simply count down that number of cards, and the card your friend selected will be at that number. (Remember, we pretended that your friend had counted down ten cards, and then cut to the ace of hearts? In that case, at the end of the trick the tenth card would be the ace of hearts.)

FREE CHOICE

I'm going to show you how to do a fine trick for two friends, and I guarantee that it'll work everytime, but I'll be darned if I know why.

Put a nickel and a penny on a table. Say to your friends, "I'm going out of the room. While I'm out, one of you decide to be a liar, and when I come back, *only tell lies*. The other of you is *only to tell the truth*. And while I'm out, you have a free choice. Each one of you pick up one of the coins — whichever you choose — and hold it tightly in your hand."

And then you, the magician, go out of the room, and your friends decide who is the liar and who is the truth-teller, and they each pick up one coin.

When you come back, point out to your two friends that they had a free choice of choosing to be a liar or truth-teller. They also had the free choice of choosing either coin. Now you give them another choice. "I'm going to ask one question. You tell me who to ask."

Your friends will decide. Then you say to the one they've chosen, "Did the liar take the penny?" (That's exactly what you must say.)

Here's the funny part of this trick. If the person you asked says, "Yes," then the other person has the penny. But if the person you asked says, "No," then he or she has the penny.

THE DANCING DIME

I've heard of having to "scratch out a living," but having to "scratch for a dime" sounds sad, doesn't it? Not in this case! If you'll scratch for this dime, it'll walk out from under a glass. Here's how the old betcha goes:

On a table covered with a tablecloth, get someone to put down two nickels. Ask that someone to place a dime in between. Now position the nickels so that the lip of a "bottoms-up" glass sits right on those 5-cent pieces.

Then say, "If I can get that dime out from

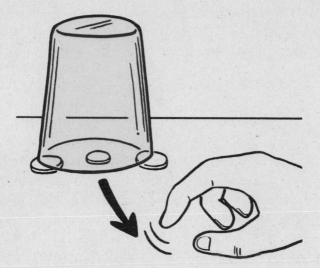

under that glass without touching the glass, can I keep it? If I can't do it, I'll give you a dime of mine!"

Your pal will probably think that's a good bet.

Then you simply scratch like a doggy trying to get a bone. Scratch that tablecloth *toward you* and the dime'll dance right out from under that glass and into your pocket!

6
Riddlers

Riddles were even popular thousands of years ago, in the days of Aesop. Of course, in those days, they weren't used for fun, but rather to decide which country would be able to tax the other and who would be king.

When Aesop was working for the ruler Lycurgus, the king of Egypt once sent this riddle to Lycurgus, "If you can send someone to build a tower high into the air — one that touches neither earth nor heaven — then you can collect three years' taxes from me. If you cannot, I will collect ten years' tribute from you."

Aesop said to Lycurgus, "Answer him, 'I will send you men to build your tower when the winter is over.'"

Then Aesop gave orders for four young eagles to be taught to carry boys on their backs. When fully grown, they would fly into the air, carrying the boys, with cords attached to them so they were under the control of the boys and would go wherever the boys wished.

Summer came, and Aesop, boys, and eagles (together with lots of servants and equipment intended to impress the Egyptians) left for Egypt. They said to the king of Egypt, "We're ready to build your tower. Point out the place." The bewildered king pointed to a field and gave measurements for the building. Aesop put one eagle at each corner of the field. The boys mounted and the eagles flew up into the air. When the boys were aloft, Aesop said to the king, "Now if you can figure out how to give them the mud, bricks, wood, and whatever else is required for the building, they are in position to start building a tower that will touch neither earth nor sky."

Of course, the king could not get the materials up to the boys and eagles who were waiting, so he lost the bet.

The Riddlers in this chapter aren't matters of life and death. Your friends will have fun racking their brains trying to figure out the answers, and you'll feel rather clever, since you were the one who asked the Riddler.

1. You have a baseball. You throw it away from you as hard as you can. It doesn't hit anything, nor does anybody catch it, but it comes back to you. There are no strings or elastics involved. Why does the ball come back?

Answer: Because you threw it up instead of forward or backward.

2. A man built a house with four sides. Each side had a southern exposure. A big bear approached the house. What color was the bear and how do you know?

Answer: The bear was a white polar bear. We know that because the house had four southern exposures. That means the house had to be built at the North Pole.

3. A man went to a movie. He found the movie so boring that he fell asleep. He dreamed that a lion was chasing him. He had a heart attack and died in his sleep. What's wrong with this story?

Answer: If the man died, how would anyone have known what he was dreaming?

4. What is it from which you may take away the whole and still have some left, or take away some and have the whole left?

Answer: The word "wholesome."

5. What is neither inside the house nor outside the house, and yet the house wouldn't be complete without it?

Answer: Windows.

6. How can you show someone what he or she never saw, what you never saw, what nobody ever saw, and which after you both have seen it, nobody else will see again?

Answer: Get a nut, crack open the shell, and take out the nut (neither of you ever saw it before, nor did anyone else). Pop the nut into your mouth and eat it (nobody will ever see it again).

7. The father is four times as old as his son. Twenty years from now, the father will be twice as old as his son. How old are the father and the son today?

Answer: The father is forty; the son is ten. In twenty years, the father will be sixty, while the son will be thirty.

8. Lying there in the yard so neat
   Was something very good to eat.
   It had neither flesh nor bone
   But in twenty-one days, it walked alone.
What is it?

Answer: An egg.

7

Are You
Crafty?

You don't have to be an expert at crafts to do these stunts. Most are pranks that just need a little something prepared ahead of time. In one case, all you have to do is make sure that you have a couple of pieces of paper and a pair of scissors handy.

A GHOST IN YOUR POCKET

This is probably a boys-only stunt, but it's so good, I don't want you to miss it.

How would you like to pull out your pocket, make a spooky move, and have your pocket return into your pants all by itself?

Here's how: Knot one end of a thread. Stick it inside one pocket, through the pants, to the inside of the other pocket. The knot will be on the inside of the first pocket, the rest of the thread will be loose inside the second pocket.

To do the trick, put in your hand and pull out the first pocket (the one with the knot in it). Show it empty and then make a few spooky moves above it. With your other hand (which is casually held in your other pocket) secretly pull in the thread. It will slowly tug that first pocket back into your pants in a weird way.

A SNAPPY TRICK

Next time you come across a handkerchief or a cloth table napkin with a hem, treasure it!

When no one is watching, push a toothpick into the hem of that hanky or napkin. Later, when you have an audience, pick up a toothpick and ask someone to break it. But before he or she

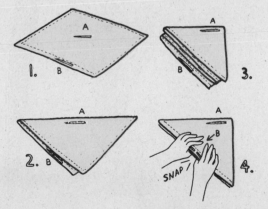

does, say, "Let me fold the toothpick into the handkerchief so no splinters will get into your palm." Fold the cloth so that the toothpick your friend actually snaps is the one pushed into the hem.

And when you open the handkerchief, your audience will see the whole toothpick lying there, unbroken and in perfect shape!

It really is a snappy trick — just don't try to do it twice in a row.

THE MOBIUS STRIP (HUH?)

Can you twist a piece of paper into a circle so that the paper only has one side? Sound impossible? Here's how:

Cut out a strip of paper like the one in the picture. On my strip, I've written #1 on one end, #2 on the other. You do the same. Turn the strip over. Behind the #2, write #4. On the other end (behind the #1) write #3. Now turn the paper back to the #1 and #2 side.

Grasp one end of the strip between your left thumb and index finger, so that your left thumb is covering #1. Put your right index finger so that it's covering #2, with the right thumb underneath (covering #3).

Twist your left thumb toward you so that it rotates and is on the bottom. Your left index finger is now on top. Twist the right hand *away* from you, so that the index finger (which was on top) is on the bottom and your right thumb is on top. Bring your two hands straight up and then together till the ends of the strip meet and then overlap, so that #3 is on top of #1. Tape in this position.

You can test whether your paper now has only one side by drawing a line lengthwise, right down the center of your circle of paper. If you have succeeded in creating a one-sided circle (which is called a mobius strip) *the line you draw will run on both sides of the paper, without your ever having lifted your pencil.*

WRITE **3**
UNDERNEATH

WRITE **4**
UNDER THIS END

JUST ONE CUT

Here's a stumper that I've never seen before. Now I'm not saying, "I've seen them all," but you should see my collection!

You can do this with your friends in school, using a piece of paper from your notebook, and instead of cutting the paper with scissors, you can tear it.

The challenge is this:

How, with just one cut, can you divide a sheet of paper into three equal pieces?

Answer: Fold the paper in half. Then fold that doubled sheet of paper into three even sections (see picture). If you make one cut — cutting off the section nearest to the fold (and cutting through the doubled sheet) — you will find that when you unfold the little section you have cut off, it will be exactly equal to the two other pieces.

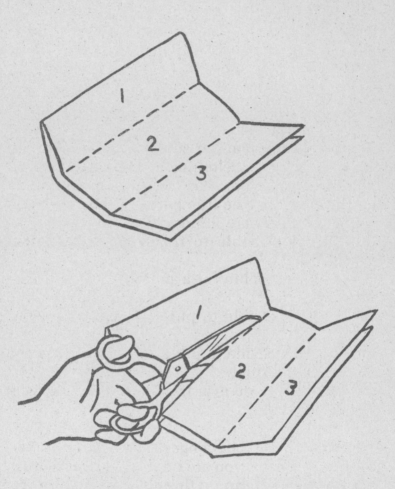

8
Impossible,
Even For You

There is an old familiar song (well, *I'm* familiar with it) that goes "Nothing is impossible, not if you dream, etc., etc., etc." Well, in my opinion, all the *etc.*'s may be true but the lyrics are not.

Lots of things are impossible.

— It's impossible to travel faster than the speed of light.

— It's impossible for a person to stay awake indefinitely.

— It's impossible to put your elbow in your mouth.

— It's impossible to put an egg together after you crack the shell.

— And have you ever tried putting toothpaste back into a tube?

Here are some challenges that have no secret solutions. Unless you are double-jointed, there's no way that you can do these stunts. But they're fun to pull on your friends, because they all sound so simple, and only you know they are impossible.

OFF THE TOP OF YOUR HEAD

A ninety-eight-pound weakling (like, say, me) can place her index finger on top of her head, and a big guy, pulling on her wrist with all his strength, will not be able to lift that finger off her head.

There are only two rules — he must not jerk the wrist (he is allowed only to pull with a steady tug) and he can't brace his elbows against his body.

NO JERKS!

Touch the tips of your two index fingers together in front of you, with your elbows out. Your friend will find that — holding your wrists, and pulling without jerking — he or she cannot separate your fingers.

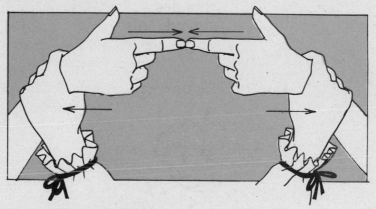

THE WEAK SPOT

Have your pal stand up. Say, "I'm going to put my index finger at a point on your face, and I promise you that you will not be able to move

forward. The only rule is this: You may not move your feet.''

And you can make good on your promise. Here's the secret: *Place your index finger sideways under your friend's nose* and keep your arm straight and stiff. It's a very delicate spot and unless your friend is a great deal stronger than you are, you'll win the bet.

TOUCH THE TIPS

Close your eyes. Stretch your arms out to the side. Point your index fingers in toward the center. Bend your elbows and bring your fingertips together without opening your eyes. Oddly enough, it's almost impossible. It's not *impossibly* impossible. I mean, I did do it a couple of times. But whether you bring your fingers together slowly or quickly, it's really hard to make the tips of those fingers touch. Your friends won't believe that this is hard until they try.

JACK CAN'T JUMP OVER THE CANDLESTICK

Here's a simple sounding but sly challenge that just can't be met:

You hold up a small object (a penny, pencil, wallet, or whatever) and say, "I'll betcha that I can put this thing on the floor in such a way that no one — absolutely no one — can jump over it. Is it a bet?" And when your friend agrees, you just put the article on the floor, *touching the wall*.

MEET YOU HALFWAY

When I'm writing stunts for a book or a newspaper column, I scribble my notes on a yellow pad and then dictate the stuff I've scribbled into a tiny dictating machine. The fun for me is watching people's faces as they hear me dictate these stunts. Invariably, their eyes start to shift, looking for whatever prop I'm talking about or their fingers rise as they unconsciously think through the stunt, doubting that I could possibly be right.

Now this next stunt is unbelievable. And as I dictated it, I saw my daughter rise, leave the room, and come back with a ruler. She just had to try it. It worked. It'll work for you, too.

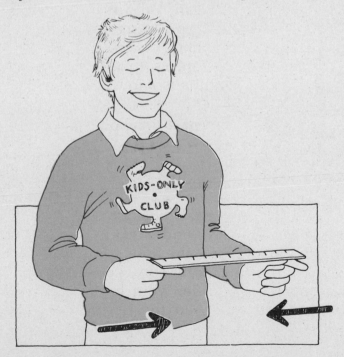

Here's what you say: "Put your index fingers under the far ends of a one-foot ruler and close your eyes. Now (with your eyes still closed) bring your fingers together. They will meet right at the six-inch mark." As a matter of fact, it's impossible for anyone to make them meet at any other point. And when the metric system really comes in full swing, and your ruler no longer reads "one-foot," your fingers will still meet smack in the middle of the stick.

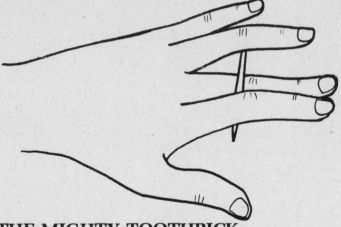

THE MIGHTY TOOTHPICK

Say to someone, "Think you're strong, eh? I'll bet you can't even break a wooden toothpick."

Then put a wooden toothpick under your pal's index finger, over the middle finger, and under the ring finger. Tell the person to keep the thumb out to the side.

In this position, it's really impossible to break that skinny little wooden toothpick (at least, I haven't met anyone who can do it). Are you a member of some splinter group that can?

KNUCKLE UNDER (#1)

Put the fingertips of your right hand so that they are touching the fingertips of your left hand. Bend in half your middle fingers (the ones between your index and ring fingers on each hand) and place them so that both middle-finger knuckles are touching (see the picture).

You must keep these knuckles together.

You'll find that you can separate your thumbs without pulling the knuckles apart — and that you can separate your index fingers and your pinkies, but it is impossible (if you keep your knuckles touching) to separate your ring fingers.

I just lied. I can do it. So can you if you're double-jointed. But if you and your pals are normal, regular people without funny fingers, you'll find that you absolutely cannot separate those ring fingers without pulling your middle-finger knuckles apart.

KNUCKLE UNDER (#2)

Have your pal place his or her hand so that the fingertips are on the table with the middle finger tucked under (see picture). Then say, "You can lift your pinkie without lifting the others, you can raise your thumb, you can wiggle your index finger, but your ring finger is very heavy, isn't it? Try to lift it. Doesn't it feel like it weighs pounds and pounds?"

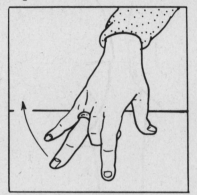

THE FINGER FAKEOUT

Think you're mixed up now? Wait until you try this stunt: Hold your arms down in front of you. Cross the wrists and clasp all of your fingers together. Bring your hands in towards your body and keep bringing them up (bending your elbows) until your fingers are on the top.

Here's the mixed up part of this stunt:

You'll now find that your fingers are so confused about where they are that they won't be able to move. Don't believe me, eh? O.K. — ask someone to point to any one of your fingers without touching it. Now you try to move that finger. No luck, right?

This is all the more amazing when you consider that you've had that finger with you all of your life!

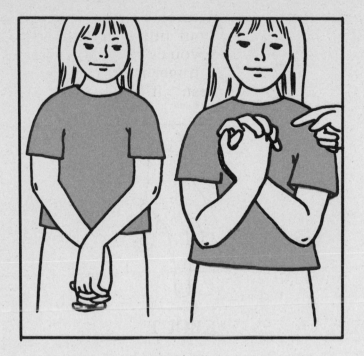

BETCHAS WITH BILLS

Here are some "impossibles" to do with dollar bills that might even have amused George Washington (although if you see his picture start to grin, get rid of that bill quickly).

Catch-a-Buck

It is impossible to catch a falling dollar bill if you do the following: Crease the dollar bill vertically (up and down) and grasp it at the top with your thumb and index finger. Now ask your friend to place one hand behind his or her back and hold the other hand so that the palm is open and next to the bill but not touching it. You drop the bill. Your friend will not be able to catch it because in the split second it takes to react the bill will already have slipped past the palm.

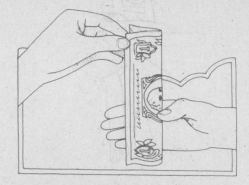

A Powerful Piece of Paper

You say, "I'll betcha you can't fix a dollar bill so that it will be absolutely impossible to tear." And when your friends get finished trying, here's what you do: Start rolling the bill from one of the corners, until the bill is tightly wound up. When it's all in a compact roll, it is absolutely impossible to tear! (Well, the Incredible Hulk can tear it, but I can't, and I'll bet you can't either.)

So Near and Yet So Far

Ask a friend to stand with heels against the wall and knees straight. Drop a dollar bill (or a ten-dollar bill, if you wish — you're safe!) right in front of the person. Now say, "If you can pick up that bill without bending your knees — just bend over, pick it up, and stand up again — you can keep it."

Don't sweat it — the money is yours.

A Buck in a Book

Since I started writing about betchas and challenges, and doing them on TV talk shows, people constantly stop me in the street and say, "Here's how I used to do it." And "it" is usually a stunt similar to one I've recently done.

The latest "here's-how-I-used-to-do-it" I was shown looks so-o-o easy — and it's really so-o-o hard. I think it's actually a "how-I-used-to-try-to-do-it" because I haven't seen anyone succeed in doing this stunt.

You put a dollar bill into a book and balance the book on end. With your hands behind your back, you stand on one foot and lean forward. The object is to try to pick the dollar bill out of the book with your teeth.

If you can get it, you can keep it — but until you actually do get it, don't bank on it.

The Blow Hard Card

Since most magicians do tricks with playing cards, I thought you'd like to learn a trick that you *can't* do with a playing card.

Start with a card from an incomplete deck. (Oh please, I beg of you, don't be a joker and use a card from one of your folks' good decks or they'll never forgive me!)

Bend the card down about ¾ inch from the edge of both sides. Stand it up on those two small ends as you see in the picture.

Now, here's the trick that can't be done. You can challenge your friends to blow as hard as they wish, but no matter how much they blow, the card will remain standing on its own two little legs! It can't be blown over.

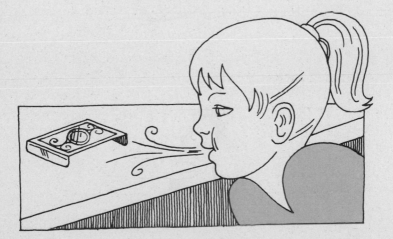

9
Pranks With a Partner

Sharing a secret is even more fun than keeping it to yourself — as long as you share it with a good friend. And your pranks will seem even more miraculous if nobody *knows* that you have a partner working with you!

SUPER SLEUTH

How would you like to be able to solve a murder mystery just like Columbo?

What will happen: While you are out of the room, somebody will pick up an object and, with great melodrama, use it as a "weapon" to pretend to "murder" one of the other people in the room.

Then the "murderer" will hide the "weapon" on any one of the other innocent bystanders and take a seat to "hide out." You, the super sleuth, will come back into the room and, without asking any questions, find the weapon, identify the victim, and correctly point to the perpetrator of the crime. (The sillier the weapon, the greater the fun. Being shot by a key or stabbed by a pillow is real melodrama.)

How it works: One of the innocent bystanders is your secret confederate. All this friend has to do is imitate the positions first of the victim and then of the criminal, and point to where the weapon is hidden — in that order.

So as you are being brought back into the room, your secret friend takes on the same position as the victim (if his or her legs are crossed, so are your friend's, and so on).

Ten seconds later your confederate changes position to match that of the murderer. After another ten seconds, your friend duplicates the way the person hiding the weapon is positioned. A final shift of the hand shows where on that person the weapon can be found.

All of this is done as you wander around the room looking into people's faces and mumbling to yourself like any good TV detective. Finally, when you've gotten all the information, with one swoop you produce the weapon, identify the victim, and accuse the murderer.

I wonder if Jim Rockford started like this?

GOOD VIBES

Oh, the groans, oh, the scorn — when I finally tell how my daughter and I do this trick. But 'til I tell, we get nothing but oohs and ahhs.

Here's what we do: I leave the room and my daughter asks someone to pick a favorite number. Then somebody else brings me back into the room. At this point, I claim that my daughter and I have close communication, and her mental vibrations will tell me the number chosen in my absence. I put my fingertips lightly on her temple and, in a moment, I name the number.

Here's how I know: As I put my fingertips on the side of her head (supposedly to get her mental vibrations) she simply tightens her jaws. This makes the muscle under my fingers press out against them. She bites her teeth together once for each number. For example, if the number is 26, she would bite her teeth together twice (indicating 2), and then she would pause and bite her teeth together six times. That's 26. She and I have worked out a code for zero: she doesn't press her teeth together and lets her jaw go slack.

SNEAKY SIGNALS

Here's a trick for you and a friend to do at your next party or Kids-Only Club meeting. It'll knock 'em out in school, too. But no one must know that your pal is in on it.

What will happen: You go out of the room, and the rest of the group picks some object in plain view of everyone. You return and various things around the room are named, one after another. When the right object is named you say instantly, "That's the one that was picked."

How does your assistant indicate the object to you? He or she doesn't. The secret of this very baffling mystery is that *you* are the one who signals. Read on.

The trick: You come back into the room and your friend starts naming or pointing to objects in different parts of the room. Four, five, or six objects are named and *when you want the selected object to be named you do something to change your position:* fold or unfold your arms, shift one foot, put your hands behind you, or any other natural and subtle movement. As soon as your assistant sees you do this, the next object he or she names must be the selected one. As soon as it is called, you announce that it was the group's choice.

Just this once, let yourself be pressured into doing the same trick twice, as the fun and frustration grow. The secret of this particular while-I'm-out-of-the-room trick is that everyone is watching and listening to your assistant, waiting for a signal that will never come.

THE WORD WIZARD

In this bit of magic, you go out of the room. Your friend asks the rest of the group to think of a word for an object. Let's suppose they decide on the word "dog."

Now you are called back into the room and in a little while you guess the selected word.

Here's how it works: When you come back into the room your friend will say, "Do you know the word?" You hear that the first word he said started with the letter D, and so you know that the word you have to guess starts with a D too. You mumble, "No," (or whatever your favorite mumble is) and your friend says, "Oh, come on, you can do it!" Now you know that the O is the second letter. When your friend urges you to, "Go on, take a guess," you've gotten the final clue, G, and you can brighten up and say, "Yes, yes, my magic powers are working — the word you selected was dog."

Arrange with the person cueing you that when the word is finished, your friend will turn his or her back on you or sit down or do some other action to let you know that *that's* the last letter of the word.

Very easy code! Very good trick!

A COIN IN A CUP

I wish I could show you this bit of magic before I tell you how it's done. Because it's so simple, you'll never believe how startling the illusion is.

You place a paper cup upside down on a table. You send your assistant out of the room and ask someone from the audience to hide a coin under the cup. You give the person from the audience a choice of four coins — a penny, nickel, dime, or quarter. When the coin is hidden, you call your assistant back into the room. Your assistant immediately tells the audience which of the four coins is hidden under the cup.

Here's how it's done: Somewhere on the side of the paper cup, you have made a tiny dot with a pencil or felt-tipped pen. When your assistant comes back, he or she simply looks for the dot. If it is facing your assistant, there is a *penny* hidden under the cup. If the dot is to your assistant's right, there's a *nickel* under the cup. If the dot is to the assistant's left, a *dime* is hidden. And if he or she cannot see the dot (because you've turned it away from your assistant and toward the audience) the *quarter* has been hidden.

10
Sneaky Petes

Sneaky Petes are easy ways to do and remember tough things. Your friends will be dumbfounded as they ransack their brains for the answers to these problems, while you have the answers right at hand.

HOW MANY DAYS?

Thirty days hath September, April, June, and November — or is it December? Frankly, I never

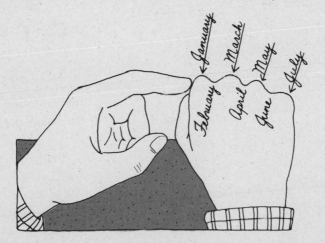

learned that little rhyme because I knew that when I wanted to figure out whether a month had thirty or thirty-one days, I always had that information handy. Not in the palm of my hand, but on my knuckles.

You do too. Hold your right hand palm down. Make a fist. See how the knuckles are high points, like mountains? And between each of the four knuckles is a low point — a valley.

With the index finger of your left hand, touch your first knuckle and call it January. It's a high point (a mountain rather than a valley), which tells you that January has the high number of days — thirty-one.

Now point to the valley next to that January mountain. Call the valley February. It's lower, so you know that it has a lower number of days (either twenty-eight or twenty-nine).

Next to February is March. A mountain. Thirty-one days again. Then point to the low valley next to March. That's April, and like all low months (except February) April has only thirty days.

And so it goes. As you can see, July lands on a mountain (thirty-one days) and from July you switch to the first knuckle of your left hand for August — which is the first mountain on the left (thirty-one days), followed by September, down in the valley, with thirty days (remember "thirty days hath September"). And when you show this amazing technique to your friends, I'll bet no one will ever fight with you about whether or not it works — because there you'll be, standing in front of them with your hand already in a fist!

NINES AT YOUR FINGERTIPS

Did you know that you can multiply by nines on your fingers?

Hold your two hands in front of you, thumbs facing one another. If you want to figure out

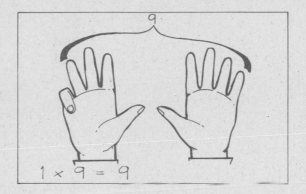

what 1 times 9 equals, bend down the pinky of your right hand. What's left is the answer: 1 times 9 equals 9 —and there are nine fingers sticking up.

For 2 times 9, bend down your right ring finger only. Again, what's left is the answer. On one side of that bent ring finger is a 1, on the

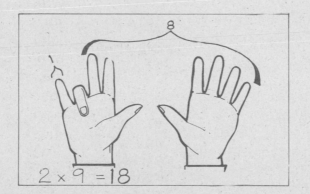

other, an 8. So 2 times 9 equals 1 and 8 — 18.

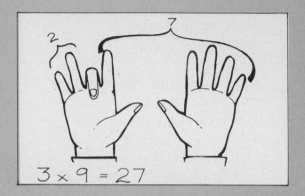

Figure out 3 times 9 by bending down only your right middle finger. To the right of that bent finger are 2 fingers sticking up, to the left, 7. So your answer is 27. That means that 3 times 9 equals 27. Is that right? Yes, that's right!

I guess you can figure the rest of it out, but it's too amazing for me to stop now! Here's 4 times 9: Bend only the right index finger down. That leaves 3 fingers sticking up to the right, 6 to the left — 36! (Which is what you get when you multiply 4 times 9, by cracky!)

A word of warning: If you do this during a test in school, your teacher will either figure that you've gone a bit strange or that you are signaling to a friend, so I suggest that you practice ahead of time and figure with your fingers in your lap.

THE "11 TIMES" SHORTCUT

Here's the shortest shortcut to multiplying any two-digit number by 11. If the two-digit number is a low one, add the two digits and plop the sum in the middle. (So, to multiply 45 by 11, just add the 4 and the 5. That gives you 9. Put the 9 in the middle between the 4 and the 5, and you have the answer, 495.)

When the sum of the two numbers is 10 or more (as it will be if you are multiplying, say, 85 by 11) here's what you do: Add the two digits together in the same way (8 and 5 is 13). Now add the first digit of the sum of those two numbers to the first number. (Take the 1 of the 13 and add it to the first number, which is the 8. That gives you 9.) Then take the second digit of that sum (13 is the sum, and the second digit of 13 is 3) put it in the middle, between the 9 and the 5. That gives 935, which is exactly what you get when you multiply 85 by 11.

11
Make Your Own
Kids-Only Club T-Shirt

If you'd like to have the Kids-Only Club design running across your T-shirt, too, here's how you can do it:

Place wax paper on top of this Kids-Only Club

design (the words are printed backwards so when you transfer this design to your shirt, they will be right). Trace it in pencil. With dark crayons, go over the outline and the details on the wax paper. Brush away any extra flecks of crayon.

Slip a shirt cardboard or small bread board inside a T-shirt to stretch the fabric a bit. Place your design *crayon side down* on the T-shirt.

Ask an adult to set the iron temperature selector for the kind of material you are using. Press the iron to the wax paper briefly (don't move it back and forth). The heat will melt the crayon and the outline will be transferred to the shirt. Take away the paper and look at what you've done.

The outline won't be sharp. Take your crayons and color in the outline and the design directly on the T-shirt, pressing hard with your crayons.

Now you have to "fix" the crayoning. With the board still in the shirt, place a fresh piece of wax paper under the shirt fabric where you have crayoned. The paper should be between the board and the inside of the shirt. Place another piece of wax paper *over* your design. Once again iron — very slowly this time — over the top sheet of the paper. The heat will melt the heavy crayoning you have put on the T-shirt, and it will really sink in.

Once your crayon colors have been ironed in, your Kids-Only Club T-shirt can be hand washed again and again in cold or lukewarm water and the colors will neither run nor fade. But don't put it in with other laundry.

Index